I DON'T LIKE GETTING OLD

CAROL LYNN LUSTGARTEN

AuthorHouse™
1663 Liberty Drive
Bloomington, IN 47403
www.authorhouse.com
Phone: 1 (800) 839-8640

Published by AuthorHouse 08/13/2015

ISBN: 978-1-5049-1067-5 (sc)
ISBN: 978-1-5049-1068-2 (e)

Library of Congress Control Number: 2015910169

Print information available on the last page.

Any people depicted in stock imagery provided by Thinkstock are models,
and such images are being used for illustrative purposes only.
Certain stock imagery © Thinkstock.

This book is printed on acid-free paper.

Because of the dynamic nature of the Internet, any web addresses or links contained in this book may have changed
since publication and may no longer be valid. The views expressed in this work are solely those of the author and do not
necessarily reflect the views of the publisher, and the publisher hereby disclaims any responsibility for them.

authorHOUSE®

I Don't Like Getting
Old

by
Carol Lynn Lustgarten

This book is dedicated in memory of my best friend, Beth Fine Kaplan who passed away at age 41 in 1998.

She will never be forgotten and always remembered! We grew up together, went to High School together and had the best of times and the most memorable of times; our Bat Mitzvah, our babysitting business, the times and adventures with the East Meadow Boys, working on our vacations at the Raleigh Hotel in Upstate N.Y., volunteer work, concerts at the Nassau Coliseum, the Marx Brothers Movies, going into New York City, getting into "trouble", getting punished, visiting each other in college, everything, you are my inspiration!!!

I will never forget you and I miss you always!!

I would also like to dedicate this book to my special aunt, Aunt Evie who passed away last year at age 90, to my brother Howard, to my mother, Rhea and to my father, David. I miss you all! L'chaim and Shalom.

Table of Contents

Pictures

Me, Beth, Karen
Carolyn's Sweet 16 Party
North Bellmore, N.Y.

Me and Brian
My Brother's Roomate from College, Texas

Ros, Me, Carolyn
Carolyn's Sweet 16 Party
North Bellmore, N.Y.

Jay's Bar Mitzvah Celebration
Florida

Beth
Boulder, Colorado

Carol + Beth
Plattsburgh, N.Y.
(college)

Me in front of my house on Queen St., North Bellmore, N.Y.

My friends, Diane, me, Janet
(In front of my house)
North Bellmore, N.Y.

At the Fine's Family BBQ

Beth, Sandy, me
North Bellmore, N.Y.

Jay (brother), me, Helene (sister)
North Bellmore, N.Y.

Lost in Movies, Memories and Lost Time

I like to get lost in movies, in memories in the early winter breeze, in my childhood and teenage years

The house on Queen Street, off Maple

That one, the first one on the right

And in the spring it had a swinging plant before you get to the front door

Sweet smell of spring, flowers in the front yard; yellow, red, pink and gold

This used to be my home

Now the new owners make it their own.

But in 1960 we used to be 5

Now, we all have separate homes

My mother, she's no longer alive

My father, no, he's not alive, he died in 2005

My baby brother, well, he died when he was 3, in 1956

My sister, she lives in Boston with her husband

My brother, he's in Rhode Island, alone

And then, there's me, I live in Queens

I moved from California in 2008 to my childhood home,

Then it was sold in 2012

That's it, that's the whole family.

I had a favorite aunt who was my mother's sister who just passed away at 90 last summer and I really miss her!

It wasn't always that way

But time creeps in, time takes the years away

There were the 70's, then the 80's left too, time crushed the 90's and now the new century is burning away

Can't fight time

Time makes history

Changes, choices, wrong place, wrong time

I choose to believe our will takes us to our destiny

I want to believe I'm only guilty of bad luck

I didn't ask for illness, it was given to me

I want to believe choices are exactly where we put ourselves in our lives

Why do some of us sometimes or mostly walk away?

Because it's easy. It always makes sense at the time.

And after it's done, we don't look back.

We don't look back or do we?

I like to get lost in movies, memories, the early winter breeze, lost time and the 70's.

This is when I was happiest, when everyone was alive.

I'll always have these times, bringing them back to life when I cross the bridges in my mind and get lost in movies, memories and lost time!

Me and Dad
Florida

Dad, me, mom
At my Aunt + Uncle's House
Wantagh, N.Y.

Dad, Jay, Mom
Albany, N.Y.

Jay, me, Mom
Rio Grand River, Mexico

The Alamo
San Antonio, TX

Me
San Antonio, TX

Me
Vanderbuilt Mansion
Centerport, N.Y.

Me
Brownsville, Texas

New Year's Resolutions

(1)   sell more books

(2)   no more crushes (I don't mean orange)

(3)   remain dateless (I don't mean the fruit)

(4)   lose weight

(5)   write more, maybe another book

(6)   go on more trips (I don't mean acid)

(7)   travel more, maybe Cuba? (Anything is possible) (Goals: Seattle, Colonial Williamsburgh) Cruise to the Eastern Caribbean, Hello San Juan

(8)   get my signals straight (I don't mean traffic) (remember the Seinfeld episode when George said to Jerry, "signals, Jerry, signals!")

(9)   no more New Year's Resolutions!

(10) go to the Green Festival in April, (2015) in New York City! I'm a Green American!

(11) and finally, make 2015 better than 2014! 2014 couldn't be any worse; I got fired in May, became unemployed, got mugged in July, my favorite aunt died in August, I was in emergency rooms in N.Y., Boston, San Francisco in 2014, I owed the IRS lots of money, (almost 2 grand) got no Hanukkah presents, had to get a crown (and not from England) (big expense) and while my brother got to go to Paris for the holidays (paid for by his millionaire friend), I just got a haircut!!
Yes, <u>2015 will be a better year</u>!!

Myra, Me, Helene
(Before Beth's wedding)
N.Y.

Helene, me, Dad
(Before Beth's wedding)
N.Y.

Family
Boston

Me and Myra
Cambridge, Mass

The Last Day of the Year

A once promising life, maybe
Going back into memories, I remember
People who were once very much alive, now gone
Dead, past horizons and cold winters
Can't be with them
Thoughts leave me cold
I'm not there yet
Now, I think, I'm without all of them,
My dead parents, my best friend, my friend, my aunt
The soldier soldiers on
My mental health recoveries, the scars
Graveyard of injuries
Memories of what they are
Ruins of time, great divides
Canyons of I
More recovery and coveted victory
A happy sanity
All for what?
What is happy?
Walking down the roads to where?

I don't want to trip over despair
There's no one there
They are all gone
I'm grateful for my sanity
Still, everyone is gone
Guess, I'm still waiting!
And it's sad to say I'm here in New York and no one is here
Everyone is gone
Hello, hello is anyone here?
It's only me,
everyone is gone ☹
Why do people say Happy New Year?

Mom and I
Epcot Orlando, Florida

Mom, me, Dad
Scituate, Mass

Me and Uncle Murray
Biscayne Bay, Florida

Jay, me, my friend, Saif
Cloisters Museum, N.Y.C.

My Art Opening at Matt Garett's
In Brookline, Mass

I think I'm going to like January

♥

I think I'm going to like January,
Walking down 67th Drive as the cold wind blows, 31°
Trees line the city streets, naked now
Sky, partly cloudy
Walking passed the old, sad Christmas trees
Tossed on the sidewalks, alone
Waiting to be taken away
Last season's decorations finally taken down, no colors, no lights
Just January sights
Coming to terms, I received no Hanukkah presents
Leave it in last year
Brutal cold
Brutal honesty
You see, there was this guy I thought
I could like
Finally getting out of my comfort zone
Did I betray myself?
I think I did
I thought I did
I poured out cold, hard honesty
Maybe too much
Maybe I got judged
I am ruined, he is ruined, we are so imperfect
I said too much, maybe the wrong things
Then I apologized
Maybe then I said the right things
He acts like a teenager, not someone 52
He doesn't mean what he says, he doesn't do what he says
I wish I could bring Sigmund Freud back to life!
So he could speak to this boy guy, this teenager, this person adrift
He needs; medication, direction, affection, inspection, correction, reflection, resurrection, attention
He needs all of this!
I need none of this, well maybe some of this
This poor guy is adrift, a miss, simply put,
        lost in the twists of his own riffs
        and doesn't get the jist of me

Out there, lost in the sea of his own tragedy!
Honestly, sinking in his Ocean of
        red bones, all alone, with white foam
                silver sand, no one to give him
                        a hand
                        the mist grips,
                tripping over pirates dreams, and green seas
                        There's nothing he can say to me! Finally!!
        Yeah, I think I'm going to like January!
                        The cold wind blows!

Me and Janet
Boston

Me and my Book, Wild Weeds
Boston

Mom, Helene, Me
Florida

Mom, Dad
Florida

Me
Walnut Creek, California

Me and Kris
Walnut Creek, California

Things You Can't Help in Life

(1) Birthdays

(2) Farts

(3) Friends who throw you under the bus

(4) Yankees who go to Seattle for money, Yankees who go to the Mets for money and Yankees who high tail it to Ohio for the money. What happened to loyalty? (What century am I living in?)

(5) bad doctors

(6) root canals

(7) rotten boyfriends

(8) People who dress in inappropriate clothes, you just want to scream, "why would you wear that in public?, didn't you look in the mirror before you walked out the door?"

(9) Stupid people

(hey, you know you can take classes at night school or online classes)

(10) people who just can't do their jobs correctly right?

(How many times did I have to return to the store and get correct change?)

People, check your receipt before you leave the store! Or I check the receipt and say whaat!!! Then I have to go back to the store, really?

(11) when you get sick, I mean really sick, some of us are not always positive, we're sick!!! Some can't be holly, jolly. You know what I mean? Then see who your friends are. Some don't stick around. ☹ (If they do, you're lucky, you have good friends.)

(12) your parents pass away

(13) getting old

(14) when people snap!

(15) when you're grown up and you thought you were gonna be this certain someone and you realize you're a nobody

(16) cheaters

(17) women who marry for money

(18) men who marry for money

(19) people who kill for money

(20) The double cross

(21) The double, double cross

(22) bad lawyers

(23) our taxes paying for guys in prison; (murderers, rapists, etc)

They get; free food, free laundry,

free medical care, free entertainment,

free work-out equipment, free toothpaste, free legal advice & counsel

That doesn't seem fair

(Things you can't help in life!)

(24) people who stone wall good ideas

(25) bad jokes

(26) nightmares

(27) being robbed

(28) arrogant people

(29) dirty old men

(30) criminals

(31) ugly criminals except for John Gotti and Michael Corleone

(32) people who lie about lying in their lying life

(33) meeting horrible dogs

(guys, you know who you are)

(34) State tax in N.Y.

(35) uninteresting Hollywood junk on the cover of People Magazine. I rather read about a story about a woman from Ohio going back to school, working 2 jobs trying to get her degree, paying her rent on meager wages, cooking her own meals & taking care of her own apartment.

And hearing about her dream in life, getting her masters and becoming the business woman with a MBA she always dreamed of. That's the story I want!!!

Not who is getting married to who.

Who cares George?

And Brad, I couldn't care less? You cheated on Jennifer. Remember, when you were married! You threw her under the bus and took up with that Miss Jolie. And Kim, do you work? What jobs have you had? I don't care how many shoes you have and all your pretty clothes, some of us want to hear about real people

You know I had 2 jobs when I was out of college. I worked 7 days a week, paid. Did you ever do that Kim? No, I don't think so.

(36) cheating men (usually once a cheater, always a cheater)

(37) dysfunctional family members

(38) very loud cellphone screamers

(39) Fraud

(40) bad drivers

(41) Bad news

(42) Big ego's

(43) bad luck

(44) Fate

(45) cheap people

(46) If you're a loser in life, then you put yourself right there. Did Charlie Manson put you there? No. Did Santa put you there? No. Did Bernie Madoff? No. Did your mother put you there? Did Oprah? Did Martha Stewart? Did Al Capone? No. You did. Don't blame anyone but yourself. Truth happens. Life is about choices. <u>Things You Can't Help in Life</u>

Me
Tulsa, Oklahoma

Me
Nantucket, Mass

Me
Beijing, China

Forbidden City
Beijing, China

Me
Maui, Hawaii

Maui, Hawaii

George and I
Grand Canyon
Arizona

Something Good

It's coming, I know it is, something good
Better than wood, better than a frozen sky
Ask me why
Something good like Jane or warm rain running down panes on my window
like a tune playing on the piano
Something good like a sunset you can never forget
I want something great that will propel us into good fortune!
Not a Soldier of Fortune, not an abortion, though that is good if you don't want the kid
Sit, don't quit, keep on writing!
Keep on driving yourself some place
Maybe into outer space, find another race
Watch with grace, with a funny face
Look at the clouds like lace, watch the waste
The pollution, chemical waters, crippled daughters
Listen to the mad captain's orders
And behind all the darkness, there will be
Something good!

Me
At The Plaka
Greece

Myra and I

Hong Kong
(If you show this True Value plastic bag in a picture at this
Hardware store in Boston, that has not been seen anywhere
in the world before, you get a $50 dollar gift card)
And I got one!

George and I
Cruise to Alaska

Me
Organized, Directed, Hosted and Acted in a Comedy Benefit for the Homeless
in Somerville, Mass

Choose Me

Stuck in years of gloom
You retreat to your room
Aching under the moon, same old routine
Walking around in dead love, poisoned long ago
Passion paralyzed, no disguise
Pools of lost faith
Sincerity cannot breathe, what do you believe?
What are your needs?
Despair hangs in the air and no one cares
Piles of deprivation
No desperation, just hunger around you
The clocks have never stopped, a collection of years
Have you been black and blue?
Who cries for you?
I haven't any glue to put you back together
There's nothing I can do
Who can justify for you?
You got to believe in something!
More than the sun and the moon
More than science and logic
More than observations and conversations
If you want to choose,
choose me, want me!

Me
Barbados

Me
The Living Desert
Desert Palm, California

Hélene and I
Boston

Me
Boston

Me and my friend, Saif on Halloween
Walnut Creek, California

Me, Jay, Helene
Queen St. House
N.Y.

Me, Dad, Jay
In the Kitchen at Queen St. House
N.Y.

I Got Played

It happened one cold January day

I liked this guy and we were friends and then I liked him more, crossed the line

That's what I said

So I called this guy and made it clear

I said, "guy," I crossed the line and I'm sorry I did, so don't call me and I won't call you, I don't like complications, it's true!"

So what does he do?

He calls me, saying, he's sorry, I feel that way

And then for weeks, he gives me double messages, plays me

I thought we were on the same page

No!

So, finally, I said, "I want to talk to you, I want to see you, you can take your anti-anxiety medication, all the drugs you need; your seroquel, zyprexa, rimeron, even morphine but you will, see me!!

But that was not to be!

He played me once again!

He said he was sick and not doing well and stayed in his little bed (at least that's what he said!)

    I think I got played once again!

So, finally I called again and left a message and said, I want to talk to you, stop hiding from me, stop avoiding me, what are you afraid of? I want to meet you, I promise I will not touch you, I will not hurt you.

    Finally, he called back and I said what do you want from me? And I finally put it out there, "Are we going to have sex before your next birthday?"

    And he said "What do you think?"

    I said "yes or no?"

He said, "we are just friends"

I wanted to scream and I did, I got played again!!!!

I said, "I don't want to be your friend, I could be friends with the bagel man down the block or my neighbor or the soap maker! I don't need someone like you so don't call me and I won't call you. And on this cold January day, I got played!!!

At the Diamond Mind in Gold Reef City
Johanesburg, South Africa

This was a horrible, painful trip in 1992. My brother was in critical condition in a car accident in Brenthurst Clinic in Johanesburg in the ICU in a coma. He was a Peace Corp Volunter and was in a car accident, while on a weekend trip in Botswana. He was flown by helicopter to Johanesburg. My family and I flew to be with him. We were by his bedside 12 hours a day except for 1 day. We decided to go to see a Diamond Mind in Gold Reef City. Eventually my brother made a full recovery!

Gold Reef City
South Africa

Florida

Uncle Irving and Aunt Rose

Me and Jay
New York City

Aunt Rose, Dad, Me, Cousin Louise, Mom
Florida

You Inspire Me

With your pretty boy looks and your charm
It appears you've got game with your walk and your name, you blow me off again and again
And I've never seen that dinner you were going to take me to, when?
I thought we were supposed to go to the movies but I went alone
Yeah, I know you were home with what's the name of your excuse?
Pleeeese!!!!!
You were suppose to call me, oh which time was that?
Come on, your nose is <u>so</u> <u>long</u> from lying, I could hang my, hat on that!!
And weren't you going to help me take pictures of my art and e-mail them to the cafe on Austin?
Yeah, right! I had to carry all 10 paintings myself, it was exhausting!
And what about the time you were supposed to meet me, you never showed and never even called
Have you ever heard of courtesy? You know we do live in the 21th century, there is technology, like a cell phone. How inconsiderate, how rude! And you didn't even try to manufacture an excuse. Disgusting!!!!

Yes, pretty boy you inspire me like a building crumbling to the ground
Like ashes turning into dust
Like metal turning into rust
Like gum getting stuck onto my shoe
As far as I can see yeah, sure, you inspire me!

Depression

Where does your depression take you?
Alone in your room
Confronting despair, nobody's there
Jesus doesn't call
And your conscience doesn't pray
But god is here, he's here for you today
What do you do with your pain and your sorrow?
Suffering madly, searching for tomorrow
Your mind is clogged, your soul's been robbed
Looking for some peace and for some passion
Hoping for some courage and for some wisdom soon
Try to face the truth, standing in front of you
But all you see is surrender!

Too Dead

Too dead to tell you
Too dead to walk down the block
Unable to take a shower, it looks like a cell block
The day is always night
but the sun somehow intrudes
There's only one feeling, one mood

Too dead to talk to anyone
Too dead to reach out, to pray
There's only darkness in the failure of my days
Too dead to read, to dream, to want, to wish, to think, to hope
Too dead to find temptation
There is no courage, no fight
                no salvation

Too dead to look for god
Too dead to see myself
Too dead to find the words that used to come
That played itself like drums
That painted so much sky
That twirled and spinned and shined
All I wanted to do was die
Too dead to live
That was I

4:19 a.m.

Left with 4:19 a.m. by my side
Sleep has been stolen, hacked away
Surrounded by darkness and the books of Emily Dickinson and Sylvia Plath
The words that comfort
That find despair and joy
That bring me up, that put me down
Sentiments
No Bribery
Foot paths to freedom, foot prints that stay forever
Now directionless in these small moments
No compass to direct me
No maps to show me back roads or tow roads
I cannot choke
Colors, I cannot catch them
The day will soon push forward and I have nothing for it
Not even a snack, not even a jar
But there will be no mist today, not a drop of fog to get lost in
Will the sun show me the way, light and remembered
But before it does, I must listen to the crickets, the turning of the tired night
The ending again, the beginning again
       anew

The ABC's for Adults

A is for Adult

    And that is what you're supposed to be when you're all grown up, so please, don't interrupt a conversation when two people are speaking and if, you absolutely must, say excuse me. Don't ever be rude. Have manners. That is what they are there for. And mind your business. Do not ask personal questions. It's not nice, you know! Have social skills; courtesy, consideration, apologize, if you are wrong, call if you will be late or are a no show and take responsibility for your actions!

B is for Butterfly

Admire this! There is so much crap in the world. Take the time to look at something beautiful.
    Maybe yourself!

C is for Cool

Be cool in all uncomfortable situations, speak up if you can. Though, only speak up in certain situations that will get you somewhere!
    Be cool!

D is for Delicious

Open yourself to the many foods the world has to offer! If you travel to many areas around the world, be open but be careful, be wise, be cautious, be safe! Try different restaurants in your area. (But always listen to your Doctor and don't ignore what the scale says)

E is for Excellent

It's all the excellent things in life you accomplished!

Congratulate yourself!

You got that job, you finished that degree, you finished making that last loan payment, you finally got that date, you got laid, you paid off that bet, paid off the IRS, you finally finished that book, you got that second job, you got that divorce, you quit that horrible job, you broke up with that crappy boyfriend or girlfriend, you moved back to N.Y., you wrote that 7th book, you had your first Improv show, got your first book published, moved again, bought your first co-op cash, walked on the Great Wall, joined the Peace Corp, got a MBA, organized, directed a Benefit Comedy show for the homeless, got that peer advocate job, finished that rehab program, made donations when you had money to different organizations, joined V.I.S.T.A. (Volunteers In Service To America) after college and worked for 1 year, did volunteer work for AIDS organizations and the homeless, went back to school at 42 after 2 degrees!

F is for Fun

Have fun in life!

Go to an amusement park, go on a ride.

Eat an ice cream cone, go to the park you decide.
Just have fun. Don't come up with excuses

G is for Great
There are <u>great</u> <u>things</u> <u>in</u> <u>life</u>.
Don't let it pass you by.
Don't be mean to people
And don't you lie!!

H is for History
We all have our history. We come with maybe sad history, complicated history, maybe bad, maybe tragedy. You are you and I am me. There will be alot that we <u>cannot</u> agree on.
But we will agree on 1 thing
We <u>cannot</u> <u>change</u> <u>History</u>.
Maybe there is happy history.
But we all have history. This is what makes us unique and individual, our history.
     Try to understand the past. It can never be changed. It is what it is, we must live with this.
     We must learn from it so we don't repeat it, we take this to the present and future and we move on and live with it and live!

I is for Ignorance
     It's a sad thing that it exists, nothing we can do but perhaps teach and educate those who do not know any better. It hurts this world, the ignorant! We can teach and educate to those who don't know any better. That's what we can do!!!

J is for Junk
I like the saying, "One man's trash is another man's treasure."
     Junk could actually turn out to be really good stuff. Some artists see junk as good stuff and create beauty from junk.

K is for Kite
Does anyone actually fly a kite these days?
     Great, if they do!

L is for Lucky
     I wish I was!
     Once I found a $100 bill on Queens Blvd. in Forest Hills and it was real!! The bank teller confirmed it!

M is for Money $ $ $
     Money screams;
     It makes the world go round,
     Bill Gates has lots of it,

people love it, people rob banks for it,
people kill for it, people marry for it,
We can't get enough of it
People dream of it, they gamble for it
      They play for it,
We can't get enough of it
Money, money, money
We love it
Like a drug
We're addicted
We're obsessed
We confess, we love our green
We're a success, if we have lots of it
      So much green
    You know what I mean
Money is our honey
    I want money
    Give me money
    Lots of money
      M is for money
        $ I love money

N is for Names
I like real names for example; Robert Zimmerman, (Bob Dylan) and Norman Jean Baker (Marilyn Monroe, Marion Morrison (John Wayne), Bernard Schwartz (Tony Curtis) Adam Yarch (MCA) Spike Jonze (Adam Spiegel), Lauren Bacall (Betty Joan Perske), Harry Houdini (Erik Weisz) Carole King (Carole Klein), Michael Landon (Eugene Oravitz), Tony Randall (Leonard Rosenberg), Mickey Rooney (Joe Yule, Jr), Meg Ryan (Margaret Hyra), Elton John (Reginald Dwight), Jason Alexander (Jay Greenspan), Joni Mitchell (Roberta Joan Anderson) Kirk Douglas (Issur Danielowitch) Cary Grant (Archibald Leach), to name a few!!!

O is for Oxygen
Without this, you cannot live,
This is a very important resource.
Everyone better work harder to protect this environment.
    Breathe in
    Breath deep
      Relax!
Take a little time
      Yourself!

<u>P is for Pal</u>

Pals aren't what they used to be.

Pals or friends could throw you under the bus given special circumstances when people get sick, pals/friends show their true colors.

My advice, always depend on yourself. People aren't who you think they are!!!

<u>Q is for Quality</u>

Look for quality made things including people in your life. It's so true. You pay for what you get.

Badly made things don't last. Get rid of bad people in your life, too!

Once you get rid of all the crappy people in your life, you'll feel a lot better!!

<u>R is for Rainbow</u>

Look for the rainbows in life!

You'll see them if you look hard enough!

Bring colors into your life!

<u>S is for Sunshine</u>

Bring Sunshine into your life when there is stormy weather!

Sunshine will give you the strength

And hope that you need

And keep it always!

<u>T is for Time</u>

The time that has gone by, that has made us who we are. From teenagers to responsible people, who we are now in our 40's and 50's and made our mistakes, learned, made corrections, took our responsibilities seriously and are middle aged. We have come to terms with some hard facts of life and still coming to terms. Some of us have lost our parents, best friends to cancer, friends to illness, family to old age, friends have faded in time, gravity has done its work on us. And father time has come to claim its place. The clock does not stop for anyone. Time keeps counting time. Marching onward, taking everyone along for the ride.

<u>U is for Understanding</u>

It's needed for everything; past, present and future.

<u>V is for Victory</u>

You may have claimed in a trying illness

You have overcome!

You have recovered!!

You declare a victory!

Let's celebrate!

YOU WON!!!

<u>W is for Winners!</u>

Celebrate everything you won!

X is for X-tra

Go the x-tra mile for someone
    Other than yourself
    Volunteer, help someone in life!
    Don't be selfish!

Y is for Yourself

Do something nice for
    yourself today!
    You deserve it!

Z is for Zoo

Go to the zoo.
See the animals,
See what they do
What do they say to you?
Watch out for that giraffe,
he may eat your shoes!!

Surrounded by Books

Here I am in the middle of it all
Surrounded by Mozart, Elton, Renaissance portraits, great French painters, New England seasons, jazz, and books
You could say this is my sanctuary, my paradise, my peace, my heaven
And I could write all night long
The day runs out of itself and the night will begin to show
August grows tired, shadows cannot sustain themselves any longer and the moon wants to take a peek
There are no feet around, just the sounds of jazz from speakers and the sights of hundreds of books around me
And the light glows, oh so happy
I feel like I'm back in school in the secluded library
That's where I went for hours and hours to study, to take in knowledge, to find more wisdom, to learn more, to find comfort, to find peace, the quiet, to create
But now, it's 1993 and now after many years,
I sit among old friends who always listen, always care
Did ya' miss me?

No Heroes

Lost in holidays, tangerines and hymn
He talks about faded bombers and faraway places
There are no heroes and there is no gold
He leaves Germany out of this and cries for France
There's so much he wants to say but the words are scattered and lost with grenades
They're buried in letters lying stiff like dust
His memories like photographs inside his head
Soldiers dressed in war, shining even in the dead of night
Every year away stamped in the palms of his hands, branded in his heart
Order, out of order,
Peering out of Sunday windows
The faceless, colorless war hangs like pictures in him!
The war still goes on in him
And the Purple Heart sits in the box in his drawer
Though, I would say in a way, he is a hero

Mr. H. H. Hallenwell

In April he looks out of his window,
into the street where sirens sound, children yell and
buses rumble up and down
Streetcars stop then they go
Mothers carry their crying babies
Outside his room nurses give out medication and
hand out love
Down the hall residents talk to no one
Some keep tapping the same old spoon,
thru all the madness
He gazes at a tree,
one he hadn't noticed before
Putting on his glasses to get a better look
He leans forward
He sees the buds of new life with new breath
The green stands out against the concrete
He shuffles to the bed,
gathers his institutional blanket
and sits back by the window
placing his cane close by
Rubbing his arthritic fingers
His eyes wander thru the tree and into the
bending branches
It reminds him of the tree in the yard where he used to live,
the one that was damaged from the storm in '56
The one his grandson used to climb,
the one he used to sit under, on warm summer nights
and think about his life
puts his head down to sleep
and dreams about spring, his past and the
new tree of life he has discovered

Days Dance

Days dance around me again and again
All the thoughts whirl in my head
Drop your defenses, there are no pretenses,
Throw away the mirrors
Talk to the Chinese girl in the shadows, she's never been the same
Throwing fortunes of yesterday away
And the tramp has lost his way in the fog,
tripped over his tattered clothes and his hair has turned gray
The politician says, "That's the price you gotta pay"
The fiddler broke his antique black bow and arrow
What a blow
All he wants to know is, where is his luck going to go
he almost got run over by the sympathy truck
The Queen sits and stares without a smile
I've walked 1,000 miles
No answers from the prophets and the lords
I want peace to sit beside me
Throw away your guns and your swords
What visions do you see?
Queen, on this day, what do you see?
Days dance around me again and again
All these thoughts, whirl in my head

Departure

Once you were admired
Even had an opening ceremony
Welcomed into this City, towering above the East river
Your structure was unique, an architectural wonder
Windows as big as plans they had for you,
the lobby like a palace
Marble as strong as you
First generation men put you together
Third generation men will pull you apart
A piece of history, now victim to demolition

This week is somber as cloud filled days become stuck
No one has consulted you on mass decision,
but somehow you knew
You stand as proud as ever though, hollowed and emptied
Choosing memories to think about instead of destruction
Your tears fall into the river, saltless and pure
Your arms reach out embracing day one last time

Morning
finally the sun crashes in,
almost causing collision
In a few minutes, you'll be gone,
some of those first generation men come to say good-bye

You will fall quick and painless,
no funerals, no flowers, no burials
Crumbling, you easily come down
Now a pile of rubble,
twisted and faceless
Soon dust will settle and cover you like a coat,
replaced by a new, modern building
One without eyes, without arms
Put together by third generation men

Once you were admired
Even had an opening ceremony
Welcomed into this city, towering above the East River
You were once an Architectural wonder
Everything gets old even beautiful buildings!
Progress has it's price ☹

Don't Forget About Me

Wish I had some rhymes
But it's only time on top of time
Things could be so handy, give me some candy
Show me how to draw, put me in awe
Look which way the wind blows, don't give me no-doz
There's the shore, there's the sea
Don't forget about me!

The sunset adores you,
Your conscience ignores you
Your negativity goes on trial
Smile for the cameras, smile for them all
You want to walk and not crawl
So here's to liberty and here's to peace!
It's the sun that's gonna light up your face,
You ignore the race
God has found you, so say some prayers
Have you sinned and will you pray?
Will it be tomorrow or will it be today?
What do you borrow and what do you wear?
Is your shirt from Jersey, is it wash and wear?
Buy a tent and camp out under the moon,
Sedated and faded, you're gonna make it soon
Drink your wine, say some rhymes
Don't pretend and don't offend
Get lots of rest and don't forget you're aging
What have you sacrificed and what do you fear?
What do you confront and what do you believe?
What have you achieved?
And remember, don't forget about me!

Robbed

Very bad experience with this bad piece of crap psycho, narcissistic fool
Played me, used me
Might as well have blown my head off with an AK 47 of deception
You little wanna be gangster
Ripped me off, got me good
You went in for the kill, got your thrill!!

Took my all, my credit cards, ID, my dignity
Went to the mall, used them all, had a ball
Went out to eat!!
You little creep, you piece of rat crap!
How many victims did you use?
I wish we could kick your ass to San Quentin and let the Big Boys have their way with you in their
cell where you belong, in hell, so long,
leave me alone, you psycho, narcissistic fool,
piece of crap
hope you get caught real soon!
And I want to see what justice will do for you!!!
Get in the rat trap, in the joint where you belong
Leave us good citizens alone!
So long, you're cruel!
Good-bye, you psycho, narcissistic fool!!!

Don't Lie to Me

Why do so many guys tell so many lies?
O.K., Shawn, you lied to me at the end of the summer,
what a bummer!!
And Trevor the liar, your pants are on fire!
You lied to me too!
And Joe, I remember you, you ripped me off for $60.
You still owe me the money, you liar!
You are a first rate cheat!
I must have been an idiot to believe you'd pay be back.
And Don, forget about you, too
Al, you lied to me about your age, you weren't 55, you were really 62!
And now you! You lied to me, too! And you knew I wouldn't go out with you
If you told me your real age!! You had to lie about being 55!
You guys, why do you lie?
Why do you think so many women can't trust most men?
Because <u>so many of you lie</u>!!!
And now, I'm really mad!!!
Do you think I'm a stupid idiot?
Don't lie to me!
If you want to lie, lie to a tree!
I caught you, guilty!
But you don't care! I swear,
go back, to your little, lying chair!
Go about your day! O.K.?
With your lying eyes, dressed in disguise!
I hope some day, someone lies to you and you feel blue, it's true!
So you know how it feels, Mr. Big Deal!
But you wouldn't care!
Because, you're just made of cheap lies put together with crappy glue and sucky alibis
Don't lie to me, you creepy guys!
If I had a dollar for every guy that lied to me,
I'd be rich as James Dean!!
Yeah, you see what I mean!
And you know exactly what I mean!
Guilty as charged!
You stink!
Strike 3!
You're out!
<u>Don't lie to me</u>!!!

1/12/15

Cool Things to do & Not Do After 55:

(1)   Go on a cruise alone
      (I went to the Eastern Caribbean (San Juan, St. Thomas, St. Maarten, Tortola - British Virgin Islands)

(2)   take short trips alone
      (Went to Rhinebeck and Hyde Park, N.Y. for 4 days)

(3)   go exploring in N.Y.C; village, Lower East side, Chinatown, solo alone

(4)   Go into art galleries, have lunch in Greek or Italian Restaurant, etc.
      Take walks in your neighborhood in beautiful spring, summer days (before the heat sets in) & autumn days

(5)   write a book, write 2 or 3 or 4 or 5 or more!

(6)   I haven't had a date or boyfriend in 2½ years (my choice) so I've had lots of free time to do great things and keep away lots of stress and liars! (I'm the author of the book, Who Needs a Boyfriend? Life, happiness & Other Thoughts.

(7)   Do a stand up comedy routine if you think you are the <u>least</u> <u>bit</u> funny at an Open Mic night (I did a routine at a Jewish Comedy Contest in Manhattan last year and I bombed. Even the Jews didn't like me, my own people! I must have been really bad! ☹) But I did get 2 chuckles when I did my ex-boyfriend material. And I was the closer! It was quite embarrassing. They had to bring on another guy to make the audience laugh after me! But I did it!)

(8)   Write in a journal

(9)   Write letters to the editor in the newspaper if you have an opinion (Everyone has an opinion) something you feel strongly about. (Though my letters since I've moved to Queens in 2012 have never been printed)

(10) <u>Buy</u> your own co-op or condo if you can afford it.
      Owning is the way to go! It's an investment! (Rent is like throwing money out the window! People said this to me when I was renting and the light bulb never went off (young and dumb). But actually, I didn't want the commitment. Now, I'm old and smart. And hey, I'm retired!)
      <u>Owning is the way to go!</u> It's all mine!

(11) If you do invest your money (which you should actually start doing at 30) I would recommend getting a broker and diversify, diversify, diversify. Never put your money in 1 stock!!!

(12) <u>For me</u>, I'll never get married!! Never have, never will, I'm not the marrying type! And at this age, never, ever! I already lived with 1 guy for 5 years, and another for 7. That's enough! At this age, you got to take care of yourself and your assets! Plain and simple!

(13) I'm not trusting at all these days so my best friend is myself. Some people can't go places, some people blow me off so I go most places alone; to the movies, out to lunch, day trips, Statue of Liberty, Ellis Island, Coney Island, 42nd St, Wall St., Union Square, exploring N.Y.C., Queens Mall, Astoria, Forest Hills (Austin St.). Even Port Jefferson on Long Island and have a great seafood dinner! It's great to be independent!

(14) <u>I could only depend on myself</u>!
      Volunteer

(15) Help an old lady across the street if she asks for your help!
      (I did this in January)
      And take her to her Apt. Building when you know she is going to need your help to get there on a cold & windy winter, N.Y. January Day!

(16) Listen to classical music to be inspired, motivated, rejuvenated, reactivated, elevated, transported, exported, supported and just plain relaxed!

(17) Don't be so trusting!! Don't be so nice! Use your judgement!
      Look at those <u>red</u>, <u>green</u> & <u>purple</u> flags!! If something doesn't seem right because it's probably not.
      (I got mugged because I didn't get away fast enough!)

(18) Don't get played!!!
      (Just be aware who is out there!)
      1. Pick up signals and double messages!!
      2. <u>Actions speak louder than words, watch patterns</u> <u>develop.</u>

(19) Become and maintain an Independent Being; by a job, your own income, your own housing, your own voice, go back to school, establish your own boundaries, have your own goals, your own support system, <u>enforce what you say you will do</u> with help from those you trust around you (all in legal ways), seek out the Legal System to help you succeed, etc. (if you need to)

(20) Do something you are afraid to do but you wanted to do for a long time. <u>Take a chance</u>, <u>make a choice</u> (<u>within reason</u>, something healthy for your life and for you!)

(21) <u>Start speaking up!!!</u> Not speaking up gets you <u>nowhere</u>!! Speaking up gets you somewhere!! <u>This is</u> <u>true</u>!!! <u>STAND UP FOR YOURSELF</u>!!!

(22) Make safe choices, <u>get</u> <u>out</u> when things aren't safe!!

Came to Confront

I want sympathy, harmony, success at it's best
My own art opening with most of my paintings sold and appreciated
I want devotion
No emotion
No one to tell me they love me
because then I have to love them back and
I don't want that
The last guy took too much from me
And back then I had to become a soldier to dodge the "mean" bullets he shot at me
I marched thru France and Poland and Bastogne, alone
And I threw the insults away like stones
I took mirrors to deflect all the jokes
And hid the hoax in big black coats
I don't know why I laughed it off with humor
I was good at that
And I cranked out justifications one by one while someone, I don't know the name of, played the drums
Then he told me, you know I sign all my cards I give you Luv purposely instead of Love, creep
He never told me he ever loved me after 1½ years
In fact, he denied a lot ever being my boyfriend
He said, "your hair looks like George Washington".
Well, at least he picked a president and he did cross the Delaware and told the truth.
They both had wooden teeth!
He would say, "Why can't you look like you, used to?"
Isn't that the ultimate insult?
I could burn myself with them in memory, again and again
But the soldier just kept marching with the bulletproof vest and the insults and meanness it did deflect
I'm not sure of the long term effects
But who could forget?

I want peace now, no pain, no insults, no war, no bulletproof vests, no bad dreams
just an easy way to go and real jokes
no one tearing at me, ripping me down
I really didn't deserve it
I should have just walked away
but I guess the sunsets kept getting in the way
Tomorrow will be better!
Tomorrow!

Train Ride

Thoughts tangled, tossed by the Hudson
Falling into autumn,
Favorite time of year
Colors of amber, gold, yellow and red
Thoughts new and old collide
Memories ride inside
There's a moral to every story
And I won't let ghosts ruin anything
Shadows are always a warning
I saw that shadow
I saw the ghost
There's a moral to every story

The train moves south, the whistle blows
We're coming thru, the rain falls
Covered in beliefs that you choose your own destiny
You must protect the very best of you
Words are just what they are
Actions speak it best
There's a moral to every story
Rain continues to fall
For every shadow, there's a wall
Riding along the Hudson
Thoughts, fall, tangled, lost in train whistles
Rain falls

Thunderstorm in Albany

Rain and rain deep
I cannot sleep
Night weeps
Stars get wet, there is a storm
Try to stay warm
Lost and tired
Are there conclusions here?
Twist and turn, yearn for the truth
We try to stay young, we try to stay strong
But what do we do with failure and weakness?
Where do they belong?
Night weeps
Stars get wet
There is a storm
Sleepless and sick
When were you born?
Count your beliefs
Save your love
Night has broken!

June

June, you strangle me with your heat and desire
At night, my room fills up with steam
I cannot breathe, I cannot dream
You're dangerous and strong
In the middle of a season
The children pray, they scream
What have you done to me?
Are you stuck in frustration?
Lost in loneliness, forced not to choose
Same routine, around and around
Crushing
Pushed to the depths of depression
Don't need to make an impression
Shining with all your imperfections
Glow in the night with all that you are
Oh June, you strangle me so, with your heat and desire
At night, my room fills up with steam
I cannot breathe, I cannot dream
Oh June!

What do You Want?

What do you want?
I just want to know
A promise, a dream or flowers that grow
An eagle, a song, a river that flows
A good luck charm, a star that glows
A sky full of gold or stories you sold
Rainbows that shine, sunsets that dance
A moon to put you in a trance
A princess who combs your hair for you
A lover who swears by you
What do you want?
Oceans to give you the truth
Rain to wash your sins away
Clouds to bury the sadness of your days
Tell me, what you want?
Do you want an elephant with a magical trunk?
Or stars to give you lots of wishes?
Or planets you can see for eternity?
What do you want from me?
I just want to know!

Still Lost in America

I don't know what he did to you and I don't know why
Did he beat you and slap you
and hit you and whack you?
Did he bruise you and make you cry?
I'm sorry for what he did to you and I don't know why
But you said you did forgive him
Is that completely true?
Did you forgive him for all he did to you?
What do you really see when you look into your father's eyes?
Are you still partly that lost little boy that never
was protected or accepted or respected?
With your mother standing by
Innocence torn away
Misunderstood and broken
Unanswered questions, words unspoken
Wounds still there, scars unable to bare at times
They NEVER leave!

Immigrant smiles and N.Y. styles, wrapped up in shiny material custom made suits for all to see
Stitch 1, stitch 2, stitch 3
Stitch 4, Tailor hands, you wanted to adore
Wanting to run past Rome, then Brooklyn became your home
Later, Queens
All you wanted was just a normal home
Alone with your thoughts and your dreams
and a language, all your own

Madonna, Mary, Jesus watching over you
The bell tolls
Say another pray
Is he standing there?
Have you forgiven him?
Have you forbidden him?
Has he asked your forgiveness?
Has he ever said he's sorry for what he has done to you and what he's put you thru?
You may be paying forever
With people and sorrow and 1000 tomorrows
I'm sorry to say

Some scars will never go away
And the people you hurt, it's ashame

So, can you crash the walls and knock your pillars down?
When will it be over?
Will it ever?

Mary has no answers
Jesus cannot say
Neither does your mother,
She doesn't know what
    to say

Find the peace you've long been after
By now, you must start finding the way
And in the end, the only things you might come
to love are the stars and Mars and the
    big and shiny Milky Way!!

Success

Jake is no fake
Wearing black leather with feathers in his hat
He speaks of dignity, pride and joy
Such a good boy
His mama is proud, his daddy sings outloud
Aunt Rose is thrilled with all her pills,
Says it makes her memory better and she can predict the weather
She does dances in the dark and has a good heart
Prays at temple on Wednesdays and makes French toast on Thursdays
Plays marbles and dominoes, visits Ohio
Rain is falling down, mama now wears a crown
Keeps it on her head until she goes to bed
Nathaniel knows it well
He's educated with a Master's, but his life used to be a disaster
Was in the Psych ward with weary books, the blues and bells
Said he went thru hell!
But helped the janitor's and the CNA's
Cleaned the Johns and made good trades
Now working 6 days a week, making poor wages
and performs on fancy stages
Learned life's lessons
Says, how life is such a blessing
Amen!

Cold February Letter

You were mean to me and I don't know why
You said mean things to me and I don't know why
I walked thru battlefields but I didn't cry
No, there were no guns, no bombs, no bullets
Oh, did you shoot some?
I couldn't see, I couldn't feel
Did I get hit?, in the back?, in the leg?, in the arm?
No, but I guess there were those scars
Why did you say those things?
Hurtful and more than a few?
I was always so nice to you
You criticized, judged, nothing was good enough for you
I know, I know
You did more for me than I did for you in the bedroom
I heard it all before
Was there a competition, I would ask?
You know, I'm not even on the Yankees
I don't even know Gardy, Tex or C.C.
I wish I did
Then maybe they can have a word with you
Then one Sunday morning, at my place after you got up, you suddenly said, "I'm going home!"
And I thought, what's wrong, what did I do?
Then the next time, when you pulled the same little stunt, "I'm going home"
I said, "oh, I'll walk you to the door and before you leave, can you please take out the garbage?"
I was 1 step ahead
Finally, this relationship, was close to dead
A relief for me
Maybe a victory for you
I can picture you, toasting a glass of wine to yourself
your winning, lonely victory under a sinful full moon, a hard rain falling
And me, I was finally free
in October, a perfect end to my favorite season!
A toast, anyone?

Can You Show Me?

I want to say nothing
I want to say everything
I don't want to get lost in the drifts, the cold, the snow and the rain
I want to know the right way to go
Can you show me?
Don't want to get lost in the mazes,
The shadows and the plays of people who walk directionless over Bridges to Nowhere
Why can't you cut down your walls and break your chains, throw your boundaries away
Why do you stay in the distance?
I'm a witness to your fears and your falls
January appears endless with
what seems to be the same moon,
The same songs, the same dreams
Orion in the sky, it's a brilliant Constellation,
Shaped as a hunter with a belt and a sword
Can you see?
Wish you can come down here and take me!

Laugh

Drive a Ford, don't get bored
Don't go far, wash your car
Clean your room, forget about doom
Go to Washington, see the senators
Don't be a predator
Eat green beans, have sweet dreams
Travel abroad, drive your Ford
Buy good things, climb big trees
Watch James Cagney
Don't let your arthritis keep you in agony
See a Joan Crawford movie, then watch I Love Lucy
Pick your dreams, stay away from disease
What is your diagnosis?
Be a good hostess
"What would you like with your steak?"
Eat a Fruit Cake
Try some cream soda with half and half
Laugh!
Take your hamburger all the way
And listen to Bob Dylan (Robert Zimmerman)
He's here to stay!

I must be Crazy

Am I thinking about you again?
Oh no, how could this be?
I must get the clouds to remove you and scatter
you in the sky
Do you wonder why?
You mean nothing to me!
How do you get into my thoughts?
Get out, right now!
Why me?
You lied to me!!
Why must I waste my precious time thinking of you?
When there's lots of things to do
Well, I could be writing more bills
or getting thrills going to my doctor or my dentist
or writing better poems than this
or writing my grocery list
You're probably just another player in the borough, got your game on
With your name on
Seeking out more bliss with your killer kisses and your capes of flirtation
with your deep desire
and your eyes on fire
trying to conspire your next hit
<u>Please</u>, don't flirt with me
and I will try dam sure not to think of you!
Oh, you guys

It's Time to Stop Acting Like a Teenager and Grow UP!!!

Just think of all the things you could do when you grow up,

You can drive a car, go to a bar, play the guitar, be a star, smoke a cigar

you can cook, write a book, stop <u>lying</u>

no more crying, no more whining

Try to be responsible!

You can take your packages to Fed-ex,

you can have sex, you can come once or twice

Have your drinks on ice, you can go to Vegas and roll the dice, eat food with spice, wear a disguise,

you can even fly the friendly skies

As a grown up the whole world is open to you!

You don't ever have to marry.

And you could go out with Peter or Larry

But you may prefer Destiny, Cindy or Mindy.

You can have lots of freedom and lots of fun. But you better follow the law and all the rules because you're a grown up now!

Be One! Be Responsible!

Think of all the things you could do!

Hey, you were born in 1962, you're no teenager you're 52!! Grow up!

Report Card on Self

A   for Reliability

B   for Truth and Honesty

C   for Commitment Issues

A   for Big Mouth - Opinionated at times, likes confrontation, only if I'm right on occasion (I look at it as educating the person)

A   for Intelligence

A   for Talents; writing, painting, cards, humor, making book marks, writing children's stories and poems, writing books, poetry, articles, prose, some Improv

D   for having hardly any friends but trying to make some (making the effort) I'm somewhat of a loner

D   for Happiness

B   for Communication Skills

A   for Independence

B   for Current Sanity

B/C   for my Current Financial Situation

B   for my Health B-making donations to (causes I believe in)

A   for Creativity

A   for Thoughtfulness

A   for Generosity

A   for Goal oriented

B   for Sense of Humor

F-   knowledge of Technology (who cares!)

A-   Having Social Skills; consideration, courtesy, empathy, sympathy, kindness

B-   Attentiveness to Others

B-   Sincerity

C-   Selfishness

B-   obsessive

D-   picking wrong boyfriends

A-   Personality

B-   Good character

A-   Faithfulness

A-   Helping others/Being supportive

B-   Listening skills

A-   Interests in Life; writing, travel, movies, music, art, trivia, reading, volunteers.

Me
Napa Valley, California

Me
Stow Lake, San Francisco

Janet, Me, Myra
Somerville, Mass

Me, Laurie
Poetry Reading
Walnut Creek Library California

Dad
At my friend Janet's wedding
Massachusetts

Family
My Father's 80th Birthday
Westbury, NY
The Piping Rock

Family
Millis, Mass

Me, Helene, Myra, Janet
North Bellmore, N.Y.

Writing at the Boston Book Fair in Copley Square
Boston
The Wild Pens

Mom and Dad

Dad, Me, Mom
At The House on Queen St. N.Y.

Family
Outside Boston

Myra, Helene, me, Janet
At Myra's Photography Exhibit
Newton, Mass

Friends, Gertie, Charlie Me and Mom
at Olive Garden where friends are family N.Y.

Me
Oxaca, Mexico

Me
Antigua

George and I

George and I
Mexico

Me

Back in Boston and back in the SNOW

Mom and Dad

Me
Portland, Maine

George and I
Alaska

Alaska

Alaska

Alaska

Australia

Melbourne, Australia

Me
Australia

Me with Mr. Horse
Melbourne, Australia

Sydney, Australia

Sydney, Australia

Mr. Kangaroo
Australia

Mr. Kangaroo
Australia

World Trade Center
October 2000

Auschwitz, Poland

Auschwitz, Poland

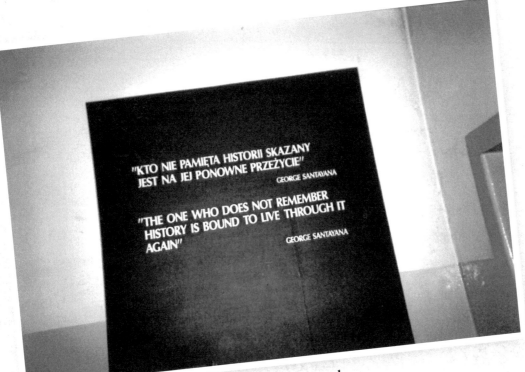

Auschwitz, Poland

Auschwitz, Poland

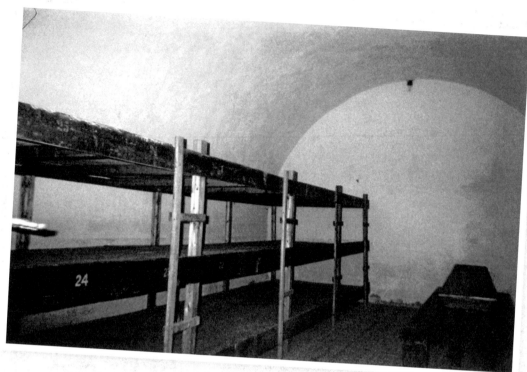

Auschwitz, Poland

Empty Cyclone B Cannister
Auschwitz, Poland

Auschwitz, Poland

Auschwitz, Poland

We will never forget

Budapest, Hungary

Printed in the United States
By Bookmasters